HAL•LEONARD
INSTRUMENTAL PLAY-ALONG

AUDIO
ACCESS
INCLUDED

PLAYBACK+
Speed • Pitch • Balance • Loop

VIOLIN

A NEW MUSICAL
WICKED

T0082061

To access audio visit:
www.halleonard.com/mylibrary

Enter Code
8112-2845-3281-5271

ISBN: 978-1-4234-4973-7

HAL•LEONARD®
CORPORATION
7777 W. BLUEMOUND RD. P.O. BOX 13819 MILWAUKEE, WI 53213

Visit Hal Leonard Online at
www.halleonard.com

AS LONG AS YOU'RE MINE

Music and Lyrics by
STEPHEN SCHWARTZ

VIOLIN

With quiet passion

DANCING THROUGH LIFE

VIOLIN

Words and Music by
STEPHEN SCHWARTZ

DEFYING GRAVITY

Words and Music by
STEPHEN SCHWARTZ

VIOLIN

Allegro, as before

mf

f

rall.

a tempo

rall.

Slower

FOR GOOD

VIOLIN

Words and Music by
STEPHEN SCHWARTZ

I COULDN'T BE HAPPIER

VIOLIN

Words and Music by
STEPHEN SCHWARTZ

I'M NOT THAT GIRL

Words and Music by
STEPHEN SCHWARTZ

VIOLIN

NO GOOD DEED

VIOLIN

Words and Music by
STEPHEN SCHWARTZ

ONE SHORT DAY

VIOLIN

Music and Lyrics by
STEPHEN SCHWARTZ

POPULAR

VIOLIN

Words and Music by
STEPHEN SCHWARTZ

WHAT IS THIS FEELING?

Words and Music by
STEPHEN SCHWARTZ

VIOLIN

THE WIZARD AND I

VIOLIN

Words and Music by
STEPHEN SCHWARTZ

WONDERFUL

VIOLIN

Music and Lyrics by
STEPHEN SCHWARTZ

NO ONE MOURNS THE WICKED

VIOLIN

Words and Music by
STEPHEN SCHWARTZ